© Copyright 2021 - All rights

You may not reproduce, duplicate or send the contents of this book without direct written permission from the author. You cannot hereby despite any circumstance blame the publisher or hold him or her to legal responsibility for any reparation, compensations, or monetary forfeiture owing to the information included herein, either in a direct or an indirect way.

Legal Notice: This book has copyright protection. You can use the book for personal purpose. You should not sell, use, alter, distribute, quote, take excerpts or paraphrase in part or whole the material contained in this book without obtaining the permission of the author first.

Disclaimer Notice: You must take note that the information in this document is for casual reading and entertainment purposes only.
We have made every attempt to provide accurate, up to date and reliable information. We do not express or imply guarantees of any kind. The persons who read admit that the writer is not occupied in giving legal, financial, medical or other advice. We put this book content by sourcing various places.

Please consult a licensed professional before you try any techniques shown in this book. By going through this document, the book lover comes to an agreement that under no situation is the author accountable for any forfeiture, direct or indirect, which they may incur because of the use of material contained in this document, including, but not limited to, — errors, omissions, or inaccuracies.

Dog Walking Log Book

Walking Log

Day	Name	Time	💧💧💧	💩
Mon				
Tue				
Wed				
Thur				
Fri				
Sat				
Sun				

Total time walked: _____

Notes:
_____
_____
_____
_____
_____
_____
_____

Highlight of the week:

Photo of the week

Walking Log

Day	Name	Time	000	💩
Mon				
Tue				
Wed				
Thur				
Fri				
Sat				
Sun				

Total time walked:_____

Notes:
_____
_____
_____
_____
_____
_____
_____

Highlight of the week:

Photo of the week

Walking Log

Day	Name	Time	💧💧💧	💩
Mon				
Tue				
Wed				
Thur				
Fri				
Sat				
Sun				

Total time walked:_____

Notes:
_____
_____
_____
_____
_____
_____
_____

Highlight of the week:

Photo of the week

Walking Log

Day	Name	Time	💧💧💧	💩
Mon				
Tue				
Wed				
Thur				
Fri				
Sat				
Sun				

Total time walked:_____

Notes:
_____
_____
_____
_____
_____
_____
_____

Highlight of the week:

_____
_____
_____
_____
_____
_____
_____
_____
_____
_____
_____
_____
_____
_____
_____
_____

Photo of the week

Walking Log

Day	Name	Time	💧💧💧	💩
Mon				
Tue				
Wed				
Thur				
Fri				
Sat				
Sun				

Total time walked: _____

Notes:
_____
_____
_____
_____
_____
_____

Highlight of the week:

Photo of the week

Walking Log

Day	Name	Time	💧💧💧	💩
Mon				
Tue				
Wed				
Thur				
Fri				
Sat				
Sun				

Total time walked:_____

Notes:
_____
_____
_____
_____
_____
_____
_____

Highlight of the week:
___

Photo of the week

Walking Log

Day	Name	Time	💧💧💧	💩
Mon				
Tue				
Wed				
Thur				
Fri				
Sat				
Sun				

Total time walked:_____

Notes:
_____
_____
_____
_____
_____
_____
_____

Highlight of the week:

Photo of the week

Walking Log

Day	Name	Time	💧💧💧	💩
Mon				
Tue				
Wed				
Thur				
Fri				
Sat				
Sun				

Total time walked: _____

Notes:
_____
_____
_____
_____
_____
_____
_____

Highlight of the week:

Photo of the week

Walking Log

Day	Name	Time	💧💧💧	💩
Mon				
Tue				
Wed				
Thur				
Fri				
Sat				
Sun				

Total time walked:_____

Notes:
_____
_____
_____
_____
_____
_____
_____
_____

Highlight of the week:
___

Photo of the week

Walking Log

Day	Name	Time	💧💧💧	💩
Mon				
Tue				
Wed				
Thur				
Fri				
Sat				
Sun				

Total time walked:_____

Notes:
_____
_____
_____
_____
_____
_____
_____

Highlight of the week:

Photo of the week

Walking Log

Day	Name	Time	💧💧💧	💩
Mon				
Tue				
Wed				
Thur				
Fri				
Sat				
Sun				

Total time walked: _____

Notes:
_____
_____
_____
_____
_____
_____
_____

Highlight of the week:

Photo of the week

Walking Log

Day	Name	Time	💧💧💧	💩
Mon				
Tue				
Wed				
Thur				
Fri				
Sat				
Sun				

Total time walked:_____

Notes:

_____
_____
_____
_____
_____
_____

Highlight of the week:
_____

Photo of the week

Walking Log

Day	Name	Time	💧💧💧	💩
Mon				
Tue				
Wed				
Thur				
Fri				
Sat				
Sun				

Total time walked:_____

Notes:
_____
_____
_____
_____
_____
_____
_____

Highlight of the week:
___

Photo of the week

Walking Log

Day	Name	Time	💧💧💧	💩
Mon				
Tue				
Wed				
Thur				
Fri				
Sat				
Sun				

Total time walked:_____

Notes:
_____
_____
_____
_____
_____
_____
_____

Highlight of the week:

_____
_____
_____
_____
_____
_____
_____
_____
_____
_____
_____
_____
_____
_____
_____
_____

Photo of the week

Walking Log

Day	Name	Time	○○○	💩
Mon				
Tue				
Wed				
Thur				
Fri				
Sat				
Sun				

Total time walked:_____

Notes:
_____
_____
_____
_____
_____
_____
_____

Highlight of the week:
___

Photo of the week

Walking Log

Day	Name	Time	💧💧💧	💩
Mon				
Tue				
Wed				
Thur				
Fri				
Sat				
Sun				

Total time walked:_____

Notes:
_____
_____
_____
_____
_____
_____
_____

Highlight of the week:

Photo of the week

Walking Log

Day	Name	Time	💧💧💧	💩
Mon				
Tue				
Wed				
Thur				
Fri				
Sat				
Sun				

Total time walked:_____

Notes:
_____
_____
_____
_____
_____
_____
_____

Highlight of the week:

_____
_____
_____
_____
_____
_____
_____
_____
_____
_____
_____
_____
_____
_____
_____
_____
_____

Photo of the week

Walking Log

Day	Name	Time	💧💧💧	💩
Mon				
Tue				
Wed				
Thur				
Fri				
Sat				
Sun				

Total time walked: _____

Notes:
_____
_____
_____
_____
_____
_____
_____

Highlight of the week:
___

Photo of the week

Walking Log

Day	Name	Time	💧💧💧	💩
Mon				
Tue				
Wed				
Thur				
Fri				
Sat				
Sun				

Total time walked:_____

Notes:
_____
_____
_____
_____
_____
_____
_____

Highlight of the week:
___

Photo of the week

Walking Log

Day	Name	Time	💧💧💧	💩
Mon				
Tue				
Wed				
Thur				
Fri				
Sat				
Sun				

Total time walked: _____

Notes:
_____
_____
_____
_____
_____
_____

Highlight of the week:
___

Photo of the week

Walking Log

Day	Name	Time	⚪⚪⚪	💩
Mon				
Tue				
Wed				
Thur				
Fri				
Sat				
Sun				

Total time walked:_____

Notes:
_____
_____
_____
_____
_____
_____
_____

Highlight of the week:

Photo of the week

Walking Log

Day	Name	Time	000	💩
Mon				
Tue				
Wed				
Thur				
Fri				
Sat				
Sun				

Total time walked:_____

Notes:
_____
_____
_____
_____
_____
_____
_____

Highlight of the week:

_____
_____
_____
_____
_____
_____
_____
_____
_____
_____
_____
_____
_____
_____
_____
_____

Photo of the week

Walking Log

Day	Name	Time	💧💧💧	💩
Mon				
Tue				
Wed				
Thur				
Fri				
Sat				
Sun				

Total time walked:_____

Notes:
_____
_____
_____
_____
_____
_____
_____

Highlight of the week:

Photo of the week

Walking Log

Day	Name	Time	💧💧💧	💩
Mon				
Tue				
Wed				
Thur				
Fri				
Sat				
Sun				

Total time walked:_____

Notes:
_____
_____
_____
_____
_____
_____

Highlight of the week:

Photo of the week

Walking Log

Day	Name	Time	💧💧💧	💩
Mon				
Tue				
Wed				
Thur				
Fri				
Sat				
Sun				

Total time walked:_____

Notes:
_____
_____
_____
_____
_____
_____
_____

Highlight of the week:

Photo of the week

Walking Log

Day	Name	Time	💧💧💧	💩
Mon				
Tue				
Wed				
Thur				
Fri				
Sat				
Sun				

Total time walked:_____

Notes:
_____
_____
_____
_____
_____
_____

Highlight of the week:
___

Photo of the week

Walking Log

Day	Name	Time	💧💧💧	💩
Mon				
Tue				
Wed				
Thur				
Fri				
Sat				
Sun				

Total time walked:_____

Notes:
_____
_____
_____
_____
_____
_____
_____

Highlight of the week:
_____
_____
_____
_____
_____
_____
_____
_____
_____
_____
_____
_____
_____
_____
_____
_____

Photo of the week

Walking Log

Day	Name	Time	💧💧💧	💩
Mon				
Tue				
Wed				
Thur				
Fri				
Sat				
Sun				

Total time walked: _____

Notes:
_____
_____
_____
_____
_____
_____
_____

Highlight of the week:
_____
_____
_____
_____
_____
_____
_____
_____
_____
_____
_____
_____
_____
_____
_____
_____

Photo of the week

Walking Log

Day	Name	Time	💧💧💧	💩
Mon				
Tue				
Wed				
Thur				
Fri				
Sat				
Sun				

Total time walked:_____

Notes:
_____
_____
_____
_____
_____
_____
_____

Highlight of the week:

Photo of the week

Walking Log

Day	Name	Time	💧💧💧	💩
Mon				
Tue				
Wed				
Thur				
Fri				
Sat				
Sun				

Total time walked: _____

Notes:
_____
_____
_____
_____
_____
_____

Highlight of the week:
___

Photo of the week

Walking Log

Day	Name	Time	💧💧💧	💩
Mon				
Tue				
Wed				
Thur				
Fri				
Sat				
Sun				

Total time walked:_____

Notes:
_____
_____
_____
_____
_____
_____

Highlight of the week:
_____
_____
_____
_____
_____
_____
_____
_____
_____
_____
_____
_____
_____
_____
_____

Photo of the week

Walking Log

Day	Name	Time	💧💧💧	💩
Mon				
Tue				
Wed				
Thur				
Fri				
Sat				
Sun				

Total time walked:_____

Notes:
_____
_____
_____
_____
_____
_____

Highlight of the week:

Photo of the week

Walking Log

Day	Name	Time	💧💧💧	💩
Mon				
Tue				
Wed				
Thur				
Fri				
Sat				
Sun				

Total time walked: _____

Notes:
_____
_____
_____
_____
_____
_____
_____

Highlight of the week:
___

Photo of the week

Walking Log

Day	Name	Time	💧💧💧	💩
Mon				
Tue				
Wed				
Thur				
Fri				
Sat				
Sun				

Total time walked:_____

Notes:
_____
_____
_____
_____
_____
_____
_____

Highlight of the week:
_____
_____
_____
_____
_____
_____
_____
_____
_____
_____
_____
_____
_____
_____
_____

Photo of the week

Walking Log

Day	Name	Time	💧💧💧	💩
Mon				
Tue				
Wed				
Thur				
Fri				
Sat				
Sun				

Total time walked: _____

Notes:
_____
_____
_____
_____
_____
_____
_____

Highlight of the week:

Photo of the week

Walking Log

Day	Name	Time	💧💧💧	💩
Mon				
Tue				
Wed				
Thur				
Fri				
Sat				
Sun				

Total time walked:_____

Notes:
_____
_____
_____
_____
_____
_____
_____

Highlight of the week:

___

Photo of the week

Walking Log

Day	Name	Time	💧💧💧	💩
Mon				
Tue				
Wed				
Thur				
Fri				
Sat				
Sun				

Total time walked:_____

Notes:
_____
_____
_____
_____
_____
_____
_____

Highlight of the week:

Photo of the week

Walking Log

Day	Name	Time	💧💧💧	💩
Mon				
Tue				
Wed				
Thur				
Fri				
Sat				
Sun				

Total time walked:_____

Notes:
_____
_____
_____
_____
_____
_____
_____

Highlight of the week:

Photo of the week

Walking Log

Day	Name	Time	💧💧💧	💩
Mon				
Tue				
Wed				
Thur				
Fri				
Sat				
Sun				

Total time walked:_____

Notes:
_____
_____
_____
_____
_____
_____

Highlight of the week:
___

Photo of the week

Walking Log

Day	Name	Time	💧💧💧	💩
Mon				
Tue				
Wed				
Thur				
Fri				
Sat				
Sun				

Total time walked:_____

Notes:
_____
_____
_____
_____
_____
_____

Highlight of the week:

Photo of the week

Walking Log

Day	Name	Time	💧💧💧	💩
Mon				
Tue				
Wed				
Thur				
Fri				
Sat				
Sun				

Total time walked: _____

Notes:
_____
_____
_____
_____
_____
_____
_____

Highlight of the week:

_____
_____
_____
_____
_____
_____
_____
_____
_____
_____
_____
_____
_____
_____
_____
_____
_____

Photo of the week

Walking Log

Day	Name	Time	💧💧💧	💩
Mon				
Tue				
Wed				
Thur				
Fri				
Sat				
Sun				

Total time walked:_____

Notes:
_____
_____
_____
_____
_____
_____

Highlight of the week:

Photo of the week

Walking Log

Day	Name	Time	💧💧💧	💩
Mon				
Tue				
Wed				
Thur				
Fri				
Sat				
Sun				

Total time walked:_____

Notes:
_____
_____
_____
_____
_____
_____

Highlight of the week:

Photo of the week

Walking Log

Day	Name	Time	💧💧💧	💩
Mon				
Tue				
Wed				
Thur				
Fri				
Sat				
Sun				

Total time walked:_____

Notes:
_____
_____
_____
_____
_____
_____
_____

Highlight of the week:
_____

Photo of the week

Walking Log

Day	Name	Time	💧💧💧	💩
Mon				
Tue				
Wed				
Thur				
Fri				
Sat				
Sun				

Total time walked:_____

Notes:
_____
_____
_____
_____
_____
_____
_____

Highlight of the week:
___

Photo of the week

Walking Log

Day	Name	Time	०००	💩
Mon				
Tue				
Wed				
Thur				
Fri				
Sat				
Sun				

Total time walked:_____

Notes:
_____
_____
_____
_____
_____
_____
_____

Highlight of the week:

Photo of the week

Walking Log

Day	Name	Time	💧💧💧	💩
Mon				
Tue				
Wed				
Thur				
Fri				
Sat				
Sun				

Total time walked: _____

Notes:
_____
_____
_____
_____
_____
_____

Highlight of the week:

Photo of the week

Walking Log

Day	Name	Time	💧💧💧	💩
Mon				
Tue				
Wed				
Thur				
Fri				
Sat				
Sun				

Total time walked:_____

Notes:
_____
_____
_____
_____
_____
_____

Highlight of the week:

Photo of the week

Walking Log

Day	Name	Time	💧💧💧	💩
Mon				
Tue				
Wed				
Thur				
Fri				
Sat				
Sun				

Total time walked:_____

Notes:
_____
_____
_____
_____
_____
_____
_____

Highlight of the week:
_____
_____
_____
_____
_____
_____
_____
_____
_____
_____
_____
_____
_____
_____

Photo of the week

Walking Log

Day	Name	Time	💧💧💧	💩
Mon				
Tue				
Wed				
Thur				
Fri				
Sat				
Sun				

Total time walked:_____

Notes:
_____
_____
_____
_____
_____
_____

Highlight of the week:

Photo of the week

Walking Log

Day	Name	Time	💧💧💧	💩
Mon				
Tue				
Wed				
Thur				
Fri				
Sat				
Sun				

Total time walked:_____

Notes:
_____
_____
_____
_____
_____
_____
_____

Highlight of the week:

Photo of the week

Walking Log

Day	Name	Time	💧💧💧	💩
Mon				
Tue				
Wed				
Thur				
Fri				
Sat				
Sun				

Total time walked:_____

Notes:
_____
_____
_____
_____
_____
_____

Highlight of the week:

Photo of the week

Walking Log

Day	Name	Time	💧💧💧	💩
Mon				
Tue				
Wed				
Thur				
Fri				
Sat				
Sun				

Total time walked:_____

Notes:
_____
_____
_____
_____
_____
_____
_____

Highlight of the week:
___

Photo of the week

Walking Log

Day	Name	Time	💧💧💧	💩
Mon				
Tue				
Wed				
Thur				
Fri				
Sat				
Sun				

Total time walked: _____

Notes:
_____
_____
_____
_____
_____
_____
_____

Highlight of the week:

Photo of the week

Walking Log

Day	Name	Time	💧💧💧	💩
Mon				
Tue				
Wed				
Thur				
Fri				
Sat				
Sun				

Total time walked: _____

Notes:
_____
_____
_____
_____
_____
_____
_____

Highlight of the week:

Photo of the week

Thank you!
We hope your experience was awesome and we can't wait to see you again soon.
As a small company, your feedback is very important to us.
Please let as know how you like our book at:

monicagopublish20@yahoo.com

CPSIA information can be obtained
at www.ICGtesting.com
Printed in the USA
LVHW050932120221
679116LV00002B/543